Some Iron Age Mediterranean Imports in England

Peter Harbison
&
Lloyd R. Laing

British Archaeological Reports 5
1974

British Archaeological Reports
122, Banbury Road, Oxford OX2 7BP, England

General Editors:

 A.R. Hands, B.Sc., M.A., D.Phil.

 Mrs Y.M. Hands

 D.R. Walker, B.A.

Advisory Editors:

 C.B. Burgess, M.A.

 Neil Cossons, M.A., F.S.A., F.M.A.

 Professor B.W. Cunliffe, M.A., Ph.D., F.S.A.

 Sonia Chadwick Hawkes, B.A., M.A., F.S.A.

 Professor G.D.B. Jones, M.A., D.Phil., F.S.A.

 Frances Lynch, M.A., F.S.A.

 P.A. Mellars, M.A., Ph.D.

 P.A. Rahtz, M.A., F.S.A.

B.A.R. 5, 1974: "Some Iron Age Mediterranean Imports in England"

© Peter Harbison and Lloyd R. Laing, 1974

The authors' moral rights under the 1988 UK Copyright,
Designs and Patents Act are hereby expressly asserted.

All rights reserved. No part of this work may be copied, reproduced, stored, sold, distributed, scanned, saved in any form of digital format or transmitted in any form digitally, without the written permission of the Publisher.

ISBN 9780904531039 paperback
ISBN 9781407322827 e-book
DOI https://doi.org/10.30861/9780904531039
A catalogue record for this book is available from the British Library
This book is available at www.barpublishing.com

SOME IRON AGE MEDITERRANEAN IMPORTS

IN ENGLAND

CONTENTS

Page

LIST OF ILLUSTRATIONS

PART ONE : INTRODUCTION   1

PART TWO : THE CATALOGUE   3

PART THREE : DISCUSSION   18

ACKNOWLEDGEMENTS   30

REFERENCES   31

LIST OF ILLUSTRATIONS

PLATES　　　　　　　　　　　　　　　　　　　　　　　　　　　after page

Ia - d　　"Rhodian" flagon fragment　　　　　　　　　　　　　5
　　　　　from Minster, Kent

IIa　　　 "Rhodian" flagon fragment　　　　　　　　　　　　　5
　　　　　from Minster, Kent

IIb　　　 Etruscan bronze oenochoe　　　　　　　　　　　　　 5
　　　　　from Northampton

III　　　 Etruscan bronze oenochoe　　　　　　　　　　　　　 5
　　　　　from Northampton

IV　　　　Flagon with trefoil-shaped mouth　　　　　　　　　　9
　　　　　from River Crouch, Essex

PART ONE : INTRODUCTION

The question of whether a number of Italic Iron Age objects said to have been found in England were genuinely imported into the country in the Iron age, or even in antiquity, has been simmering quietly since the publication of the Italic bronze skillet and jug from the Aylesford cemetery in 1890.[1] These were the first reliably authenticated pre-Roman Italic finds to have been discovered in Britain, but that they were by no means the only ones was made clear by Ridgeway and Smith, who read a paper in 1906[2] drawing attention to a considerable number of Italic fibulae housed in English and Scottish museums and bearing British provenances. The authors pointed out that not a single one of these fibulae could be conclusively proved to be a genuine Iron Age import, and suggested that while it was nevertheless likely that a number of these brooches had reached England in ancient times, there were probably many others which had been given British localities to enhance their value.

By the time the next - and more comprehensive - survey came to be compiled by D. B. Harden in 1950,[3] the number of English brooches of Italic and other foreign origins dating from the ninth to the fourth century B.C. had swollen to a surprising total of 78. Harden was able to show that with few exceptions, the findspots of these fibulae were confined to South-Eastern England, a fact which would be surprising if all of them were modern losses, or even Roman imports. He noted, too, that it would be unlikely that modern collectors would have concentrated entirely upon Italic fibulae without inadvertently allowing some Greek examples to slip into their collections. Harden's survey also included a number of bronze vessels and Greek or Italiote pottery as well as coins, many of which he regarded as genuine, but at the same time he wisely in our view rejected the authenticity of some of the pottery finds. Harden argued that there was a "remarkably large group of these things which do not seem capable of being explained as Roman imports, and are, equally, not found in places where they would be likely to be dropped by modern collectors". The Aylesford bronzes, he continued, "leave no grounds for disputing that at least a large proportion of the others are genuine pre-Roman imports". Despite a concentration of coins in South-Western England, he argued for their arrival in England by a land-route across the Alps and down the Rhine, rather than by a sea route direct from the Mediterranean.

More recently, one of us (L. R. L.) discussed pottery and coins largely from the West Country in relation to a possible Greek tin trade with Cornwall.[4] Most of the pottery found in the South-West was regarded as dubious, though a kylix from near Reading (Catalogue No. 5, below) was accepted as genuine. On the subject of coins, Laing stated that "we can say with some confidence that some of the Greek coins from Britain are modern losses, some came here in Roman times, and a few very probably are Iron Age losses". He adverted to the fact that the distribution of Greek coins coincided much better with that of the imported pottery than with that of modern collectors, thus strengthening the argument in favour of the genuineness of some of the finds.

In this monograph, some significant but unpublished items of pottery and bronze are presented in some detail, and are placed in chronological order alongside some of the already well-known material, even if the genuineness of some of it is in doubt. Although unequivocal accounts of the circumstances of the finding of the items presented here for the first time are not always forthcoming for purposes of authentication, it is argued that the genuineness of a number of them is strengthened when considered against the background of the pattern of Continental export and distribution - of which nineteenth century dealers and collectors knew little or nothing. This same pattern helps to distinguish the ancient from the modern losses amongst the other finds listed in the Catalogue in Part Two, as we believe that a number of finds can be rejected because no other examples of the type have been found outside the Mediterranean. Using this criterium, certain finds which have been accepted as genuine by others have been dismissed as spurious by us.

PART TWO : THE CATALOGUE

1. Proto-Corinthian Bowl (Skyphos)   Winchester, Hants.
   Circa 700 B.C.
   Present location: Winchester Museum
   Circumstances of finding: 'Found in Winchester'

This vessel is in buff ware with a band of geometric painted decoration below the rim. The only reason for supposing that it was found in Winchester is an entry in the 1853 Winchester Museum Catalogue, describing it as an 'Athenian vase, found in Winchester'.[5] Nothing further is known about it, and in view of the fact that Proto-Corinthian pottery was not extensively traded outside the Mediterranean area, it can almost certainly be regarded as a stray from an eighteenth or nineteenth century collection.

   Authenticity: Very doubtful

2. Italic Cup   Barn Elms, near London
   7th century B.C.
   Present location: British Museum, London
   Circumstances of finding: Said to have been found in the gravel on the banks of the Thames[6]

This pottery cup with upstanding handles is already well-known, as it has been published a number of times. However, with regard to the genuineness of the find, Professor Hawkes has pointed out to us in a letter that the gravel in which it is said to have been found may have been brought from the Pool of London by the Thames Conservancy Board, so that in theory the cup could have come from anywhere. It is almost certainly a modern loss.

   Authenticity: Doubtful

<u>3</u>.   "Rhodian" Flagon Fragment (Pl. I a-d, IIa)   Minster, Kent

   <u>Late 7th/Early 6th century B. C.</u>

   Present location: City Museum and Art Gallery, Birmingham
   Cat. No. 687'53

   Circumstances of finding: Not recorded

This unpublished fragment was presented to the Museum in Birmingham by Mrs. Edith Prentice in 1953. It was reported to have been found at Minster, but no further details are available.

It measures 9.1 cm. wide by 7.5 cm. high, and has an overall black colour composed of a basic oxide patina with some light green and blue carbonate corrosion products.[7] The surviving fragment, which appears to be hollow cast, consists of the handle attachment with disc terminals, decorated with an ornamental palmette. The handle itself is missing.

The fragment formed part of a so-called "Rhodian" flagon - a type discussed by Jacobsthal, particularly in the light of those found in Hallstatt graves north of the Alps.[8] He pointed out that these flagons were found not only in Italy, but also at Vilsingen[9] and Kappel[10] in South-Western Germany, and Pertuis (Vaucluse) in France.[11] There is a further unprovenanced example in the Musée Borély in Marseilles and another in the Musee de la Ville in Vienne in the Rhône valley,[12] though doubts have been expressed about the French provenance of the latter piece.[13] Den Boesterd has published an unprovenanced handle of a similar flagon from the Kam Collection in Nijmegen.[14] Doubts surround the origin of many of the items in this collection, but while there is nothing to prove that the handle may have been found in the Netherlands, the alleged discovery of the handle fragment in Kent at least makes its Dutch provenance less unlikely. Camporeale has recently listed two further examples from Vetulonia,[15] and we can now add two newly-published Spanish examples - one from Huelva and the other bought in Granada around 1900.[16] For Jacobsthal, these flagons were probably of Rhodian origin - hence the name - and were datable to the first half of the sixth century B. C. But Frey has demonstrated that they are not Rhodian but were manufactured in Etruria,[17] and he also pointed out that they date from the last third of the seventh century till at least the first quarter if not the first half of the 6th century B.C.[18] We will scarcely go far wrong if we date our Kentish specimen to the same period.

The find circumstances of this fragment shed little light on its genuineness. The fact that very few items of Italic origin were being traded northwards across the Alps, and that practically none of these other than fibulae can be proved to have reached England by the middle of the sixth century B.C. would not argue in favour of the find. Nevertheless, the discovery of other "Rhodian" flagons in southern Germany, does show that these vessels were being traded over the Alps, thus making their presence in southern England possible, if not necessarily likely.

Authenticity: Possible, but by no means certain

4. <u>Corinthian jug</u>　　　　　　　　　　The Medway, near Chatham
circa 550 B.C.
Present location:　?
Circumstances of finding: Found in the bank or the bed of the Medway in 1871

This Corinthian jug dating from around the middle of the 6th century B.C. was exhibited by Mr. Leggett at the Society of Antiquaries in London in 1935.[19] Mr. Leggett said that his father had seen it being dug up during extension work at Chatham dockyard in 1871. Although the information about the discovery of the jug is more precise than in many of the other cases catalogued here, the almost complete lack of Corinthian pottery from genuine archaeological contexts north of the Alps suggests that the find be labelled as a likely modern loss.

Authenticity: Likely to be a modern loss

5. Greek Kylix　　　　　　　　　　Thames, near Reading
Late 6th century B.C.
Present location: Reading Museum
Circumstances of finding: Said to have been dredged from the Thames, probably somewhere near Reading

Boon published this Attic red-figure kylix by the Pithos painter in 1958,

PLATES Ia - d

"Rhodian" flagon fragment from Minster, Kent (Catalogue no. 3)

Ia (upper left)   :   Rim, front view (length 9.1 cm.)

Ib (upper right) :   Rim, top view

Ic (lower left)   :   Rim, back view

Id (lower right) :   Rim, underside

Photos: Birmingham Museum

PLATES IIa - b

IIa : "Rhodian" flagon fragment from Minster, Kent (Catalogue no. 3): Terminal disc.

Photo: Birmingham Museum

IIb : Etruscan bronze oenochoe from Northampton (Catalogue no. 7): Anchor termination of handle.

Hunt Collection. Photo: Ian Finlay

PLATE III

Etruscan bronze oenochoe from Northampton (Catalogue no. 7)

Hunt Collection. Photo: Ian Finlay

although it had been purchased by the Reading Museum as far back as 1896.[20] As the lime deposit on its surface corresponds to that on other riverine finds, there would thus appear to be no good reason to doubt that this kylix was genuinely dredged from the Thames.

    Authenticity: Probably genuine

6.   <u>Magna Graecia Terracotta</u>   <u>Nutbourne, Sussex</u>
    <u>circa 500 B. C.</u>
    Present location: Formerly in Worthing Museum, but lost during the last war
    Circumstances of finding: Ploughed up in a field

Harden was the first to publish this terracotta, which is now, unfortunately, lost.[21] It is in Ripe Archaic style, and is attributable on stylistic grounds to a workshop in Magna Graecia, probably Sicily.[22] Greek terracottas are prized by collectors, and have never been found in Europe outside Hellenized areas, as they were not traded. This should probably be regarded as a collector's stray.

    Authenticity: Probably a modern loss

7.   <u>Etruscan Bronze Oenochoe</u> (Pl. IIb, III)   <u>Northampton</u>
    <u>Late 6th/First half 5th century B. C.</u>
    Present location: Collection Mr. and Mrs. John Hunt, Baily, Co. Dublin
    Circumstances of finding: Old label on the neck states "Oenochoe found at Northampton 1864 from J. P."

This oenochoe may have come either from the Ball collection in St. Albans, or from a Northamptonshire collection sold at Sotheby's probably before the last war. The vessel is 24.5 cm. high, and has a maximum diameter of 14.5 cm. It is thus one of the more squat examples of its type, with a broad body leading in a gradual curve to a wide neck; the mouth and spout rise gradually in the same plane. The handle, which is attached by a rivet, is of crude workmanship and belongs to the common type with anchor termination at the lower end and with a pointed bulbous termination at the mouth. The flattened rim of the spout and the body near the lower end of the handle have both been slightly damaged. Much of the surface is covered with a greenish-white patina which is partly disintegrating.

The classic work on such vessels is by Jacobsthal and Langsdorff, who demonstrated an Etruscan origin for them and suggested a date in the first half of the fifth century B.C.[23] Again it was Frey who indicated that the importation of these oenochoai into the area north of the Alps had already begun in the second half of the sixth century B.C.[24] The late sixth century grave from Hatten in Alsace[25] contained an oenochoe with a handle very similar to the Northampton specimen, but, as Frey pointed out, the simple anchor termination had a long life, and can thus be early or late. If we are to rely on the typology suggested by Szilágyi[26] whereby the mouths and beaks of earlier vessels are on two different planes, whereas those in the later series are in a straight line, then the Northampton example would be somewhat later in the series. But the Hatten oenochoe shows that this typology is not watertight. It should not be forgotten that the French grave from Somme Bionne in the Marne shows that oenochoai were still in use if not actually still being manufactured as late as about 420 B.C. We must leave the date of the Northampton flagon an open question, but it is likely that it would belong with the majority of its peers in the first half of the fifth century B.C., if not a little before.

The Museum and Art Gallery of the County Borough of Northampton have no knowledge of the discovery of the vessel. Not even the initials J.P. given on the label attached to the neck can be identified. W. Robert Moore, the Museum's Archaeological Assistant, has informed us, however, that there was a John Phipps who was mayor of the town in 1862, magistrate in 1864, an Honorary Curator of Fine Arts, Prints and Etchings in 1884 and a member of the Northampton Museum Committee from at least 1884 until 1889. John Phipps may have been the person whose initials appear on the label, but this is pure speculation, as we have no further information other than that provided by the label.

A number of Roman items came to light sporadically at and around a quarry at Duston on the outskirts of Northampton for some years after 1859, and the suspicion could arise - particularly in view of the absence of any other pre-Roman material from the site - that an attempt may have been made to associate a modern collector's piece with finds from Duston. But, as against that, all the finds from Duston were published in 1871 by Sharp[27] - the man who had gathered and had helped to collect them - and he made no mention of any bronze vessels from the site, so that this suspicion may be dismissed. But as a great number of oenochoai were exported from Etruria to areas north of the Alps (see Discussion, below) there is nothing inherently improbable in the Northampton oenochoe having reached England in Iron Age times. Certainly the continental distribution of oenochoai discussed below on page 21f. provide us with no compelling reason to dismiss the evidence of the label that the specimen under consideration really was found in Northampton.

    Authenticity: Probably genuine

8.   Flagon with Trefoil-shaped Mouth (Pl. IV)   River Crouch, Essex
    First half 5th century B. C.
    Present location : Chelmsford and Essex Museum, Chelmsford.
        Inv. No. B. 18563
    Circumstances of finding: Found in the bed of the River Crouch in 1912 by Mr. I. Fripp, of Hockley, and donated to the Museum by R. G. Williment, Brentwood, on November 7th, 1933.

This Etruscan flagon with trefoil-shaped mouth is now round-bottomed, but it must once have had a ring-foot attached to it on which it stood. Its present height is about 21 cm. The greatest circumference is high up on the body of the vessel, and a short shoulder glides over to the neck with its trefoil-shaped mouth. The lower termination of the handle is formed by an egg motif, below which there are anchor-like terminals and a palmette. The surviving upper termination has a sitting lion with upright head, and in the centre is another lion's head whose mane runs back down the handle. A certain amount of uncertainty exists in the Museum's records as to whether the handle belongs, as it has been re-mounted since the vessel came into the Museum's possession. It may have been confused with a (Roman?) handle from Dunmow - the provenance at present given for it on the card in the exhibition case. However, there is a strong likelihood that the handle does belong, as other vessels of the type with somewhat similar handles are known from Italy.

The only other complete bronze vessel with trefoil mouth known to have been found north of the Alps is that from Hatten.[28] But Giessler and Kraft published a further mouth fragment from Gundlingen near Freiburg,[29] and J.-P. Mohen has kindly informed us of the existence of the lower part of a globular vessel with lions on the handle which was probably found at Menet (Cantal) and which is now in the Musée des Antiquités Nationales in St. Germain-en-Laye (Inv. No. 31.651). But as we have not seen this French specimen, we are not in a position to judge how far is compares with the River Crouch flagon. The Hatten jug has a large flat base, and generally has a form differing from that of the River Crouch vessel, the only feature common to both (other than the shape of the mouth) being the presence of the lion's head at the top of the handle. However, the best parallels for both handle and body of the River Crouch flagon are found in Italy, although their findspots are by no means always known. The handle terminating in the seated lion with head erect is paralleled in certain unprovenanced pieces discussed and illustrated by Brown,[30] but their stems are more faceted than that of the River Crouch example. The only comparison for the egg-like motif above the palmette is on a somewhat stockier unprovenanced handle illustrated by Babelon and Blanchet.[31] The body of the River Crouch jug belongs to a series of vessels discussed by Magi;[32] whilst most of these have the more constricted mouth typical of the oenochoai, some have the broader mouth seen in the Essex jug. The body-shape and lion handle are combined in a vessel from Vulci illustrated by Schumacher,[33] though here the sitting lion is replaced by a simple lion's head. A vessel from Cumae[34] has a slightly taller neck, and a belly rather than a shoulder; its handle, though more faceted than the River Crouch one, does bear the egg motif and has seated lions, but between these there is a palmette, and there are rams' heads on the lower termination of the handle. While we can find no exact

PLATE IV

Flagon with trefoil-shaped mouth from River Crouch, Essex (Catalogue no. 8).

Chelmsford and Essex Museum.   Photo: Douglas H. Crome

parallel for both vessel and handle together, we may accept that both represent an Etruscan type which Brown says is 'mostly of the first half of the fifth century',[35] and it is in this half century that we should probably place the manufacture of the River Crouch jug.

Although almost 20 years elapsed between the alleged discovery of the vessel in the River Crouch and the recording of its discovery when it was donated to the Museum, there is no strong reason to doubt its genuineness, particularly in view of the fact that other vessels with trefoil-shaped mouths are known to have been traded across the Alps. Its coastal location facing the Continent, and its proximity to the Thames estuary where a number of other imports are known, can only strengthen the argument.

    Authenticity: Probably genuine

9.   Statue of Turms   Uffington, Berkshire
    circa 480-460 B.C.
    Present location: Ashmolean Museum, Oxford
    Circumstances of finding: Said to have been found at Uffington over a century ago

This statuette of Turms has already been published by Riis.[36] He attributes it to the Vulci school, and suggested a date in the seventies or sixties of the fifth century B.C. It is almost certainly a collector's piece, as statuettes were never traded.

    Authenticity: Very doubtful

10.   Cordoned Situla   Weybridge, Surrey
    5th century B.C.
    Present location: British Museum, London
    Circumstances of finding: Found in a gravel deposit under 4 metres of sand and clay

This situla is already so well known[37] that it need only be mentioned in passing here. The type has been discussed in detail recently by Stjernquist[38] who show its distribution to extend to France, Belgium and elsewhere. The

Belgian example at Eygenbilsen[39] dating from the fifth century B.C. is presumably contemporary, and lends obvious weight to the genuineness of the Weybridge find.

    Authenticity: Almost certainly genuine

11. <u>Four Red-Figure Attic Lekythoi</u>   <u>Halamanning, Cornwall</u>
    <u>5th century B.C.</u>
    Present location: ?
    Circumstances of finding: No details recorded

Four funerary <u>lekythoi</u> are reputed to have been found at Halamanning, Penwith, in Cornwall.[40] The find is immediately suspect as lekythoi were made for graves and never traded. Investigation shows that they came from the collection of a man who bought most of his antiquities in London and afterwards ascribed them to local findspots. Halamanning was a farm he used to visit frequently.[41]

    Authenticity: A modern hoax

12. <u>Three Pottery Vessels</u>   <u>Teignmouth, Devon</u>
    <u>4th century B.C.</u>
    Present location: Torquay Museum
    Circumstances of finding: said to have been found together in an
                                  artificial cave at Teignmouth

Of these three vessels which can be attributed to the 4th century B.C., one is an Attic drinking cup of bolsal shape, black-glazed and dating from the second half of the century. The second is an oenochoe with trefoil mouth in light grey ware and partial red glaze, which could conceivably be even slightly later than the 4th century. The third is a two-handled bowl, similar in fabric and glaze to the oenochoe.[42] Nothing further is known about the find other than what is stated above, but it would not appear that these three vessels constitute a modern loss. The fact that all three are types which were in use systadially in the East Mediterranean might support the theory that they are a genuine association. Not enough was known about Hellenistic pottery in the nineteenth century to 'fake' a group like this.

Authenticity: Probably genuine

13. Bronze Jug   Tewkesbury, Gloucestershire
    4th century B.C.
    Present location: British Museum, London Inv. No. 1903.2-14.1
    Circumstances of finding: Not recorded

The British Museum Guide to Early Iron Age Antiquities[43] illustrated this bronze jug with high standing handle. It stands 13 cm. high from base to rim, the handle rising further to give a total height of 17.5 cm. It is in poor condition, most of one side of the jug being missing, and the green and brown surface being rough and crumbling. It belongs to a type of Etruscan jug with free swung handle (for hooking on to a support) which dates from the fourth century B.C. and which has parallels from Vulci and from Certosa di Bologna.[44]

    Authenticity: Genuineness possible, but not very probable

14. Bronze Jug   Bath
    4th century B.C.
    Present location: Bath Museum
    Circumstances of finding: Not recorded

This is a jug similar in type and date to that from Tewksebury (No. 13, above), though differing from it in that its handle terminates in a hoof.[45] The attribution of location is on the basis of an old label. As someone in the last century may have attempted to pass it off as Roman, thinking that Bath would be a suitable provenance, the genuineness of this find should be looked upon with considerable suspicion, particularly in view of the fact that no other examples - other than the possible specimen from Tewkesbury - are known north of the Alps, and also in the light of the almost total disappearance of Etruscan exports northwards in the 4th century B.C. (see below, pages 21, 25f.)

    Authenticity: Probably spurious

15. Twelve Greek Vessels   Selsey Bill, Sussex

6th - 2nd century B.C.

Present location: British Museum

Circumstances of finding: Three separate finds, not well documented. Two were made by a fisherman, the third by Heron-Allen who published them[46]

On three occasions groups of vessels were found in the same place at Selsey Bill. A large number are lekythoi or squat lekythoi, which like those from Halamanning (Catalogue No. 11, above) were made for graves and not traded. Although some of the vessels, such as an Ivy Leaf lekythos and a Palmette lekythos, are types which are frequently found together in graves of the mid fifth century - as can be seen from Graves 431 and 353 in the N.E. Cemetery at Corinth[47] or Grave 453 at Olynthus[48] - the chronological range of the whole Selsey Bill group is very wide. The earliest dates from the late sixth century B.C. and the latest, a lamp of Broneer's Class XII, dates from the late third or early second century B.C.[49] Presumably they were deposited together, and could have been a collector's discarded haul. It is noteworthy that they were nearly all bad specimens, and are all of a type a collector might have acquired on a visit to Sicily.

Authenticity: A modern loss

16. Three Greek Vessels   Dorchester-on-Thames

4th century B.C.

Present location: Ashmolean Museum, Oxford

Inv. No.	Type of vessel
1921.172	Skyphos
1921.173	Small Oenochoe
1893.168	Stemless cup

Circumstances of finding: Skyphos and small oenochoe both have their provenance given as Dorchester on old attached labels, and were originally in the hands of a Mr Ogden. Both are from the Manning collection.

> Stemless cup given to the Museum by Mr.
> William Cozens of Bishop's Court,
> Dorchester, and said to have been dug up
> in the rickyard of Manor Farm, Dorchester.

These vessels have already been published and illustrated by Harden.[50] The skyphos belongs to Type 595A at Olynthus[51] and is datable to the second quarter of the fourth century B.C., while the black-glazed oenochoe or olpe of the same date or slightly later belongs to type 326 at Olynthus.[52] The stemless cup has a red fabric and lustrous black wash, and can be ascribed with reasonable confidence to the fourth century B.C.

Although these finds cannot be disregarded entirely, it is perhaps necessary to be cautious in accepting them as ancient losses. Manning, from whose collection two of the items came, was a well-known local antiquary, and we need not doubt that he believed his finds to be genuine. But Dorchester at the time was well-known on account of the current excavation of the Roman settlement, and a dealer wishing to increase the value of his merchandise would naturally assign as a findspot a well-known archaeological site.

Authenticity: Possibly spurious

17. <u>Attic Lamp</u> <u>Shotover, Oxford</u>
    <u>First half 4th century B.C.</u>
    Present location: Ashmolean Museum, Oxford   Inv. No. 1923.666
    Circumstances of finding: Said to have been found at Shotover and given
    > to the Museum by Mr. T.S. Bott, who had
    > found the piece among the effects of his
    > grandfather who had worked on the Shotover
    > Estate

The lamp, of Attic black ware, belongs to class 23C in the Athenian agora series[53] or Broneer's Class VI.[54] It dates from the first half of the fourth century B.C., and was mentioned by Harden.[55] The find must be suspect as lamps were never traded very extensively. They were designed for burning olive oil, which would also have had to be traded. Dr. Anthony Hands has kindly informed us that Shotover was the site of considerable Romano-British activity, with a North-South "main road" running by the western foot of the hill, and with pottery kilns and a supposed "small settlement" on the western slope of the hill. It is quite likely that someone may have tried to attach the findspot Shotover to a lamp imported into England in the last century, and in any case the fact that the earliest recorded owner of the lamp worked at Shotover need not necessarily imply that it was found there.

    Authenticity: Probably spurious

18.   Delphini Type Lamp   Sandy, Bedfordshire
     Late 4th/mid 3rd century B.C.
     Present location: Ashmolean Museum, Oxford   Inv. No. R.311
     Circumstances of finding: Said to have been found at Sandy in 1862, and donated to the Museum by Sir Arthur Evans in 1907

This lamp of so-called delphini form is of a type which was current in Athens from the late fourth to the mid third century B.C.[56] Sandy is best known for its small Romano-British settlement. For reasons given above under Catalogue No. 17, this is probably to be regarded as a modern loss.

    Authenticity: Probably a modern loss

19.   Three Greek Lamps   London
     Hellenistic
     Present location: Formerly in Bethnal Green, now in the Guildhall Museum, London
     Circumstances of finding: Two are said to have been found together in Queen Street in London, and the third is said to have come from the Chaffer collection

All three lamps are Hellenistic. One has a lime incrustation upon it of a type commonly found in the Eastern Mediterranean, particularly on objects from Cyprus.[57] All three are probably modern losses.

    Authenticity: Probably modern losses

20. Squat Lekythos   Great Chesterford, Essex
    4th century B.C.
    Present location: Formerly in Warrington Museum, Lancashire[58] but lost since the war[59]
    Circumstances of finding: None recorded

This squat lekythos dating from the fourth century B.C. came from a nineteenth century collection, along with Roman pottery and other finds from Essex. Great Chesterford was made famous in the nineteenth century by R.C. Neville's excavations there, and would obviously be a convenient name for a dealer's story.

   Authenticity: Probably a modern loss

21. Miniature Hydria   Barking Creek, London
    4th/3rd century B.C.
    Present location: Guildhall Museum, London
    Circumstances of finding: Found at Barking Creek in 1932, supposedly at a depth of 15 feet

This miniature hydria is usually ascribed to the sixth century B.C., but it is probably Hellenistic.[60] It shows traces of a lime deposit of the sort noted above (Catalogue No. 19) as being characteristic of objects unearthed in the Eastern Mediterranean region, though it is possible that such a lime deposit could well have been acquired from the mud of the Creek. It is almost certainly spurious.

   Authenticity: Almost certainly spurious

22. Arrowhead with the Monogram of Berenice   River Kennet near Reading
    3rd century B.C.
    Present location: Formerly in Reading Museum, now in the British Museum, London   Inv. No. 1954.9-12.1
    Circumstances of finding: Found by a fisherman on the end of his hook while he was fishing in the Kennet near Reading

The tang and the barb of the arrowhead are missing. It has a bluish patina. It is of bronze and bears the monogram ⌶. Haynes, in studying this type of arrowhead, identified the monogram as that of Berenice II of Egypt, who ruled in the absence of her husband Ptolemy III in Syria, 247-222 B.C. He suggested that she had a band of Cretan mercenaries whose arrowheads bore her monogram.[61] There are arrowheads from Cyrene and Knossos in the British Museum of the same general type and with the same monogram,[62] and one is recorded from France.[63] The discovery of the Kennet piece seems well authenticated, and it is not entirely beyond the limits of possibility that it came to Britain (with a soldier of fortune?) in the Early Iron Age.

Authenticity: Quite probably genuine

PART THREE : DISCUSSION

The Problem of Authentication

The normal reaction to such imported finds as those listed above is to deny that they are genuine Iron Age imports, and to suggest that they were brought here either by the Romans or by much more recent collectors returning heavily laden from their Grand Tour. But the comparatively large number of finds, including fibulae and coins, should make us consider seriously if many of them are not in fact ancient imports. Collectors, after all, are among the more possessive members of the human race, and are scarcely likely to be throwing rare items from their collections into rivers or burying them in fields. Dealers, on the other hand, are not above attributing false findspots to items otherwise without provenance in order to enhance their value. In the case of objects with a classical appearance, even if they date from centuries before the Roman invasion, the attribution to a findspot from whence Roman material is known to have come would be quite a natural one for an unsuspecting and possibly not very knowledgeable collector. This may well have been the fate of items like the Dorchester skyphos and oenochoe (Catalogue No. 16), the Shotover lamp (Catalogue No. 17), the Great Chesterford lekythos (Catalogue No. 20) and the Bath jug (Catalogue No. 14).

Obviously one of the best ways to check on the authenticity of a find is to look into the circumstances of its finding. Unfortunately, only very few cases provide us with any kind of satisfactory details. The Corinthian jug from the Medway (Catalogue No. 4) was at least observed when being excavated, although the details were not published for more than half a century. The discovery of the Weybridge situla (Catalogue No. 10) and the Kennet arrowhead (Catalogue No. 22) were apparently adequately recorded too, as was also the hydria from Barking Creek (Catalogue No. 21). The patina of the latter piece, however, helps to cast a certain doubt on its authenticity, while the only other apparently adequately recorded find - that of the Nutbourne terracotta (Catalogue No. 6) - is unlikely to have been a genuine Iron Age import as such items are not known to have been traded outside Hellenized areas. So that even where the find circumstances have been recorded, a certain amount of doubt must still remain. As can be seen from the details given above, some of the alleged provenances are based upon old labels, like that of the Northampton oenochoe (Catalogue No. 7) or two of the pottery items from Dorchester (Catalogue No. 16). In the majority of cases, the objects are merely 'said to have been found' - and it is with these, and with the objects where no details of the discovery have been recorded at all, that a certain amount of scepticism is most obviously justified.

In the absence in all but a few cases of adequately recorded details of the discovery of these objects, there is another line of approach which can very often help in suggesting that a find is not genuine. This is to study the distribution of the type to which the object in question belongs. Obvious examples are the lamps (Catalogue Nos. 17-19) which are not found outside the Mediterranean, and which can therefore be excluded from the 'genuine' list almost immediately. The same argument helps to exclude the Proto-Corinthian skyphos from Winchester (Catalogue No. 1), the Nutbourne terracotta (Catalogue No. 6), the Turms statue from Uffington (Catalogue No. 9), the Halamanning lekythoi (Catalogue No. 11) and the pottery from Selsey Bill (Catalogue No. 15). Nevertheless, this argument cannot be applied too rigidly, for if the Kennet arrowhead (Catalogue No. 22) did not have reasonably reliably recorded find circumstances, it could well have been put in the 'doubtful' category, although it must be admitted that another similar arrowhead is known from France. Using the same argument, the Tewkesbury (Catalogue No. 13) and Bath (Catalogue No. 14) jugs should probably also be excluded, though it could be argued that they were genuine because two similar types had been found in such comparatively close proximity to one another and because Tewkesbury is not a provenance which a dealer would be likely to attach to a jug of its kind. The case of the three vessels from Teignmouth (Catalogue No. 12) is not easy to decide, for although the three vessels belong to types not normally found outside the Mediterranean, the fact that all three are of much the same date makes it somewhat unlikely that anyone was trying to perpetrate a hoax with them in the last century, when knowledge about dating was not as refined as it is today. The hydria from Barking Creek (Catalogue No. 21) is a type also found only in the Mediterranean, and is unlikely to be genuine because of its patina, despite the fact that the hydria is one of the few items where find circumstances have been recorded.

There are, however, a number of items which cannot necessarily be excluded from the 'genuine' list, and which must be examined, because they belong to types which were or could conceivably have been traded across the Alps and down the Rhine to England. When we look at these finds against the background of the Continental distribution of the types in question, it becomes neither archaeologically impossible nor even unlikely that many of them were imported into Britain during the Iron Age and were genuinely deposited in England's soil or fell or were thrown into her rivers shortly after importation. To deal adequately with the question, we must now turn to the Continent for comparison.

The English finds in their European setting

From the seventh to the fourth centuries B.C.[64] a very considerable number of objects, particularly Etruscan, were imported into Central Europe from the Mediterranean lands. The find from Kastenwald, near Colmar[65] demonstrated that Italic bronze vessels began to trickle northwards from Etruria as early as the seventh century B.C.[66] This increased to a more regular stream in the late seventh/early sixth century B.C. with the importation of Perlrandbecken and Etruscan "Rhodian" jugs[67] like that from Minster (Catalogue No. 3). The hydria from Grächwyl in Switzerland has recently been dated to 580/570 B.C.[68] and Cahn[69] has given us details of later Swiss imports. Millotte[70] includes the tripods from La Garenne and Ste. Colombe[71] and other items in his list of French imports of the sixth century B.C., most famous of all of which is the great krater from Vix.[72] Both Vix and Hatten[73] demonstrate that oenochoai and other Mediterranean vessels including one with trefoil-shaped mouth were being buried in Western Central Europe by the last quarter of the sixth century B.C. A very considerable amount of Greek Black and Red Figure pottery of sixth and fifth century date has been found north of the Alps,[74] and Dehn has shown that the innovation of wheel-turned pottery was spreading northwards from the Mediterranean world in the late Hallstatt period.[75] The Conliège amphora[76] can be dated to the late sixth or early fifth century B.C., and Kimmig has shown that the Rhenish situlae were beginning to come from the Ticino area northwards to the Middle Rhine at about the same time.[77] By the fifth century B.C. there was a veritable torrent of bronze vessels pouring into central Europe from Etruria, many of them probably connected with wine for feasts. In this context we can recall the words of Posidonius describing the Celts:

> 'the drink of the wealthy classes is wine imported from Italy or from the territory of Marseilles'.[78]

The most numerous of these vessels are the oenochoai[79] of the same type as the Northampton vessel, and the majority of these are normally dated to the first half of the fifth century B.C. Schaaff[80] has recently listed the Central European basins with heart-shaped terminals and the stamnoi or stamnoi-situlae which were probably imported from Etruria during the same century. The great flow is again reduced to a trickle in the fourth century, when the Waldalgesheim bucket[81] seems to be one of the few finds to show that Italic imports were being sent northwards into Central Europe at this time.

The great majority of these imports got little further north than the Marne, the Middle Rhine and Bohemia. Indications are not, however, lacking to show that some broke through this cordon and penetrated further northwards. On most distribution maps of oenochoai, Eygenbilsen in Belgium stands alone and isolated north of the Middle Rhine. But Tröltsch[82] mentions a lost example from Kempen, Kr. Dusseldorf, and another - now also lost - from Mook in the Dutch province of Limburg. The fact that both of these are lost should not mean that we should reject them completely as never having been found. The Kam collection in the Rijksmuseum in Nijmegen contains two oenochoai handles, one from Hunerburg near Nijmegen, the other unprovenanced.[83] The same collection includes among its material of unknown origin not only the handle of a "Rhodian" jug mentioned above, but also a bronze basin which appears to have interlace on the rim[84] and which may belong to a class of vessels whose origin goes back to Etruria.[85] However, it should be pointed out that while the Hunerburg handle may genuinely have been found in Holland, we should place no reliance on the unprovenanced pieces in the Kam collection as they could have come from anywhere. It might also be mentioned here that a Hallstatt burial with a four-wheeled waggon found at Wijchen in Gelderland[86] belongs to a grave type otherwise little represented north of the Middle Rhine, except for that from Havelter Berg, shortly to be published by Dr. Verwers. Professor Dehn has also kindly drawn our attention to what may be Greek pottery which has recently come to light at Kemelberg in Belgium.[87] While not all of these finds are authenticated, there does however seem to be evidence that Etruscan imports penetrated northwards down the Rhine and practically reached the shores of the English Channel. The cordoned situlae studied by Stjernquist[88] and the Greek cauldron from Langaa in Denmark[89] show indeed that Mediterranean imports really went much further north on the Continent.

If these Etruscan objects got to the verge of the Continental shore of the English Channel, the question can well be posed why they could not have crossed the Channel to England? Up to the end of the fifth century, the English bronze vessels and at least some of the pottery would seem to be a natural extension of the more northerly Continental outposts of Italic export markets. That these Etruscan objects could have come to England over the Alps and down the Rhine to Holland and then across the Channel rather than by any other route could be backed up by the predominantly south-eastern distribution of the finds in England, a distribution pattern confirmed by Harden for the fibulae.[90] A very similar pattern can be observed with the Coptic bronze vessels a thousand years later.[91] Almost certainly the same trade route was employed later in the Iron Age, for along it travelled the bronzes of 'Ornavasso' type to Aylesford and Welwyn, which will be discussed again below.

At this point we may briefly consider some of the Italic brooches from the British Isles. The majority of these brooches date from the ninth to the seventh century B.C. and belong not to a study of imports in Early Iron Age England but rather to a study of the Atlantic Bronze Age. There are over eighty such brooches recorded, with a distribution mainly in the South-East.[92] Special mention may be made here of a few brooches of Certosa type, which belong to the late sixth and fifth century B.C. There is one from Trumpington, Cambridge,[93] another from Tinker's Hill, Finkley, Hants., now in Reading Museum,[94] another from Cumberland[95] and yet others from Ixworth[96] and Icklingham.[97] As can be seen, these are rare in comparison with the other types of earlier date. Particularly interesting is the find from Ixworth, which has produced numerous brooches (a fact which is, in itself, suspect) and also a fragmentary embossed bronze bowl rim with horsemen in Hallstatt D style of the sixth century B.C.[98] One should not overlook, in the same context, that Hallstatt double-spiral and allied brooches are not unknown in Britain - they have been noted from London, Ixworth and Colchester[99] - though the types represented are mainly early. That Hallstatt D objects were reaching Britain from the Continent in the sixth century B.C. is substantiated by the iron antenna dagger from the Thames at London,[100] the 'Nut' moulded neck or arm rings from Clynnog in Caernarvonshire,[101] Co. Antrim[102] and Scarborough,[103] or in Scotland by the series of Hallstatt imports associated with the Covesea, Adabrock and Tarves phases of Coles' sequence, in the period from 700 B.C.[104] For Halstatt C in England one might cite the Llyn Fawr hoard[105] or the razors of Staple Howe type.[106]

Still on the subject of brooches, there is a curious 'group' from Alton, Hants. This consisted of a Late Serpentiform brooch of Sundwall's Class HII. The precise type is not easy to parallel, but typologically a date in the mid-seventh century seems not improbable.[107] It was found along with a plate-footed leech brooch belonging to Sundwall's Class BIIIg 5[108] which would give it a chronological horizon of circa 725-675 B.C. They were together associated with a scarab of XXVI Dynasty, i.e. 663-525 B.C. and some pottery, now unfortunately lost.[109] They were found while workmen were excavating for material to build a mound in the grounds of an asylum. The dating of the three finds is remarkably close, though one is a little too early perhaps to be associated with the scarab. It is noteworthy that from the XXVI Dynasty come a whole series of scarabs which were traded extensively and which were found in Greece. That some reached Etruria is proved by the fact that they occur in tombs - Egyptian contact was already established in the time of Bocchoris (720-715 B. C.), and a faience vase and seal of his have been found in an Etruscan tomb.[110] Remarkable as it is, the Alton find should probably be dismissed. In the same way, a later and large Ptolemaic basalt statue of a priest found 8 or 9 feet under clay during excavations at Hayes, Middlesex[111] is probably equally to be dismissed, as such statues were not apparently traded any great distance.

On the whole, certain of the English finds of the seventh to the fifth centuries B. C. catalogued above follow the Continental pattern very closely, and this may be used as a further argument for their authenticity. The Winchester skyphos (Catalogue No. 1) and the Barn Elms cup (Catalogue No. 2) would both appear to lie before the horizon in which Greek pottery was imported into Central Europe, and can probably be dismissed for this reason. The Corinthian jug from the Medway (Catalogue No. 4), although its discovery appears to have been adequately observed, would also seem to be slightly too early to be accepted as a part of the stream of pottery exported over the Alps in the sixth century B. C. The fact that it is Corinthian as opposed to the customary Black (or Red) Figure pottery would also speak against its genuineness. The "Rhodian" flagon from Minster (Catalogue No. 3) is certainly just early enough to have been a genuine import, and its authenticity can be strengthened by the knowledge that others of its type were exported northwards over the Alps to Southern Germany. However, the long geographical gap intervening between Southern Germany and the Kent coast, taken together with the fact that imports of the late seventh or early sixth century B. C. are very rare would suggest that we should only accept the Minster flagon with a certain slight reservation.

The situation is different, however, with the Attic red-figure kylix from the Thames, near Reading (Catalogue No. 5), the Northampton oenochoe (Catalogue No. 7), the River Crough flagon (Catalogue No. 8) and the Weybridge situla (Catalogue No. 10). They all conform to a pattern of Etruscan exports to Central Europe from the late sixth to the end of the fifth century B. C., and although the Northampton oenochoe was found further inland than might have been expected, we could probably accept these finds as genuine Iron Age imports. It would seem that the inhabitants of Britain at that time were not going to be outdone by their Central European brethren in the importation of Etruscan bronze feasting vessels. It might be mentioned in passing that a small bronze statuette which is alleged to have been found in Sligo in the last century and which was published by Jacobsthal[112] as being Iberian, is probably Etruscan and dates to around the third quarter of the seventh century B. C. Such statuettes were apparently exported to France, where one from Thorigné-en-Charnie[113] provides the closest parallel. If the Sligo statuette were to be accepted as a genuine import - and it is not easy to do so - then possibly even Ireland was receiving its imports from Etruria too.

Dehn[114] has recently suggested that transhumance may have been partly responsible for a number of Etruscan objects having been bartered and subsequently finding their way northwards over or around the foot of the Alps, but this argument can scarcely be evoked for England. The most likely explanation of these English imports before 400 B. C. is that they were the result of adventurous merchants or their central European partners continuing the trade in Etruscan bronze vessels down the Rhine and across to England. They may, however, have been presents given to forge a bond,[115] or it may be that the inhabitants of south-eastern England wanted to keep up with or imitate their Continental peers by celebrating the same feasts as would appear to have taken place in the Rhineland, though they do not appear to have buried the objects in graves after death as was the Central European custom. We have, however, very little evidence for burial custom in England in the seventh to the fifth century B. C. - if we can judge by the possible waggon grave excavated at Beaulieu Heath in the New Forest,[116] there must have been a few burials at least imitating the Continental.

With the advent of the fourth century B. C. the picture changes completely. The Campanian situla from Waldalgesheim is the only southern import of the period found in Central Europe (see footnote 81). By this time, Etruscan products are no longer traded across the Alps and down the Rhine. In consequence, South-eastern England had to do without its Etruscan vessels. For this reason, the Tewkesbury (Catalogue No. 13) and Bath (Catalogue No. 14) jugs are not likely to be genuine, though the authenticity of the Tewkesbury example cannot be entirely excluded. If either were genuine, it would suggest that late Etruscan exports were reaching Britain's shores by a route other than that down the Rhine.

It is our view that with the possible exception of the Teignmouth 'cache' (Catalogue No. 12), the Kennet arrowhead (Catalogue No. 22), and - less likely - the Tewkesbury jug (Catalogue No. 13), none of the Greek and Italic finds dating from after 400 B.C. found on the English side of the Channel and catalogued above are in fact genuine losses in antiquity. The most probable explanation for most of the finds of Hellenistic pottery is that they were brought back by sailors and then discarded. Many have been found near ports. Collectors, on the whole, do not throw away items from their collections, but prefer to sell them.

The finds of Greek coins belong to a different category of evidence. The coin evidence has already been reviewed by one of us.[117] Although many of the recorded finds are undoubtedly strays from collections or other recent losses, and others represent arrivals in Britain during the Roman occupation, some at least appear to have been lost in antiquity, as is most clearly demonstrated by the find of a coin of Ptolemy V (204-181 B.C.) stratified with pottery of Iron Age Southern Second B character at Winchester.[118]

An analysis of the coin finds suggests two things. First, few if any of the Greek coins in the British Isles need have reached these shores before about 280 B.C. at the earliest. Secondly, there is a marked concentration round the mouth of the Thames, in the Isle of Wight and along the neighbouring south coast. On the basis of this and other evidence it can be suggested that some of the coins were traded, possibly as ornaments, by way of the traditional 'Tin Trade' routes. The distribution of coins and other material on the Continent suggests that such trade with the Mediterranean was conducted by several routes, notably the Seine-Rhône, the Loire-Rhône or the Garonne-Aude. It is likely that the second was the oldest route, the Loire being apparently used even in the Late Bronze Age[119] while the southern route was probably little used - Greek coins are rare in the Languedoc, except near the coast.[120] The northern route was probably in use in the Roman period.[121]

The last phase of imports in Iron Age Britain begins with those from the 'Y' grave at Aylesford, the Bronze Plated Situla grave, which belongs to the Middle phase of the Aylesford culture. Dr. Birchall, in reviewing the high chronology usually put forward for the Aylesford cemetery, has been able to demonstrate that the Middle Period graves, i.e. the Bucket Graves, must now be assigned to the period circa 50-10 B.C.[122] The 'Y' Grave at Aylesford contained a jug and patera which can be paralleled by finds from the Ornavasso cemetery in northern Italy, and the dating of these vessels can now be established through the re-assessment of the date of the graves in this cemetery and through subsequent finds in Italy. The particular types of bronzes found at Aylesford should probably be assigned to the period 30-20 B.C., as associated with them was a brooch also of Ornavasso type datable to the Augustan period.[123]

The bronzes of Ornavasso type have been well studied in Europe by Werner,[124] and seemingly similar vessels to those from Aylesford enjoy a wide distribution north of the Alps between about 50 B.C. and the time of Drusus' campaigns on the Rhine about 12 B.C. and the time of the submission of the Vindelici in 15 B.C. After this date these types are replaced by Campanian cast forms and their derivatives. The distribution of these Ornavasso vessels follows the rivers, notably the Rhine, and it is probably by way of the Rhine that they passed northwards, spreading down into Gaul and across to Britain by way of the westerly trade routes related to the westerly Belgic movement.[125] The pattern is a repeat of that seen for the trade of Etruscan bronzes some centuries earlier.

The Ornavasso type of bronzework has been found at Welwyn, where an Ornavasso jug was found with a cremation burial in the 'A' grave and a jug and patera in the 'B' grave. The notable absence of any Gallo-Belgic pottery from Welwyn and the similarity of the pottery from Aylesford would suggest that the finds from the two sites are contemporary.[126] The Welwyn patera has a degenerate palmette on the bottom of the handle, which ends in a kind of swan's head, as it does on the Aylesford patera. Apart from the parallel at Ornavasso, the Welwyn patera can be compared with vessels from Hammau and Nienbüttel in Germany.[127] The jug had a swan's head handle attachment, and was probably of Campanian origin.

Related to the Ornavasso bronzes but later than them are the series of Campanian cast forms and their derivatives. These broadly speaking fall into two categories, Swan's head paterae and Dolphin situlae. They were to travel far beyond the frontiers of the Roman Empire in the early first century A.D. and indeed even by the end of the first century B.C. some had penetrated as far as the Vistula and the Passarge, one reaching Sweden.[128] Fragments of Dolphin situlae are recorded from near Colchester and from Surrey.[129] To the same general class of bronzes belong the situlae with human masks on the attachments for the handle loops, which also seem to have been manufactured in Campania and which enjoyed a distribution which is essentially Central European, with outliers in Poland, Denmark and Sweden.[130] A mask from such a situla, depicting the head of Silenus, was found outside Colchester in 1845 and has been assigned on stylistic grounds to the Augustan or Julio-Claudian period.[131]

Wheeler, in studying the trade patterns of these Campanian types of vessels, has demonstrated that by the time of Augustus they were being traded via Carnuntum to Bohemia, where the Marcomannic king Maroboduus encouraged the activities of Roman traders. From here they were traded north and west to the Low Countries.

Although the finds are limited in Britain, it can be seen that they are all restricted to the south-east. The explanation probably lies in the fact that they were traded from Gallia Belgica by Belgic middlemen. It may be noted, as Hodson has emphasised, that the pottery of the Middle Period graves at Aylesford and Welwyn shows affinities with vessels from Northern France and the Low Countries.[132] These early finds should be regarded as status imports, and not part of a symposiastic outfit.

With Welwyn we come on to a series of imports of all types associated with chieftain's graves. These have recently been well studied by Stead, and we need not discuss them further here.[133] Nor, in this discussion, is there any need to consider the later Belgic imports in Iron Age Britain - the majority are imports from Gallia Belgica and were probably the products of provincial workshops. They have, for the most part, been well published. It is not until the beginning of the Roman period that we see again objects of ultimately Mediterranean origin appearing in British contexts.

Conclusion

Other writers have accepted many of the items catalogued above in Part Two as genuine Iron Age imports, but certain of these have been largely rejected by us on the grounds that they were otherwise not traded outside the Mediterranean. We suggest that only a handful are likely to be genuine, for although their find circumstances are often inadequately recorded, they fit into a pattern of Etruscan exports northwards across the Alps in the sixth and fifth centuries B.C. If they are genuine Iron Age imports - as we believe they are - they suggest that the South-East of England was at the end of a long trade route which went northwards across the Alps from Etruria and then down the Rhine. Only two, or at most three, of the finds dating from after 400 B.C. are likely to be genuine, and of these, the two most likely ones are not of Italian but of Eastern Mediterranean origin. They date from a period when the export of Etruscan wares northwards had almost come to a standstill.

ACKNOWLEDGEMENTS

We should like to acknowledge here the help we have had from numerous museums and individuals in compiling this study. We are particularly indebted to Birmingham Museum, in particular to Dr. Joan Taylor and Mr. Nicholas Thomas, for information about the Minster jug and for permission to publish it. We should like to express our thanks also to Mr. and Mrs. John Hunt for their permission to publish the Northampton oenochoe, to J.-P. Mohen for information on items in the Musée des Antiquités Nationales in St. Germain-en-Laye, and to Professors W. Dehn, Marburg, and O.-H. Frey, Hamburg, and to Drs. V. Pingel and G. J. Verwers for help in connection with the Continental material. Our thanks are due also to Dr. D. B. Harden, Miss Cherry Lavell, Messrs Jarvis and Jones of the Chelmsford and Essex Museum, and W. R. Moore of the Northampton Museum for assistance in a number of ways. We are also indebted to Reading Museum, the Guildhall Museum, the Ashmolean Museum, the British Museum and the Chelmsford and Essex Museum for permission to publish specimens in their collections and for information about them, and also to the Winchester Museum for information about their skyphos. We are also grateful to the Warrington and Northampton Museum for information relating to material from Great Chesterford and Northampton respectively. Finally, our thanks to Professor T. G. E. Powell and Professor O.-H. Frey for having read through the text in draft and for having offered useful suggestions, and to British Archaeological Reports for having kindly agreed to publish this work.

REFERENCES

1. Evans, A. J. 'On a Late-Celtic Urn-Field at Aylesford, Kent, and the Gaulish, Illyro-Italic, and Classical Connexions of the Forms of Pottery and Bronze-work there discovered', Archaeologia 52, 1890, 315-88.

2. Ridgeway, W. and R. A. Smith in Proc. Soc. Ant. London 21, 1906-07, 104-06.

3. Harden, D. B. 'Italic and Etruscan Finds in Britain', in Atti del 1º Congresso Internazionale di Preistoria e Protohistoria Mediterranea, Firenze-Napoli-Roma, (1950) 315-24. Harden has pointed out to us that two of the objects from the Castor find mentioned on p. 318 as having been post were seen in Peterborough Museum in 1967. The Billingsgate rhyton has turned out in the meantime to be a modern forgery - see Bailey, D. M. 'A so-called Greek Rhyton from London', Antiquity 33, 1959, 218-19.

4. Laing, L. R. 'A Greek Tin Trade with Cornwall?', Cornish Archaeology 7, 1968, 15-23.

5. Information about this object kindly supplied by Winchester City Museum.

6. British Museum Guide to Early Iron Age Antiquities (1925), 90, with Fig. 88; Waddington, Q. 'Vestiges of Pre-Roman London', Journ. British Archaeol. Assoc. 39, 1934, 384 and 398, Fig. 5; Harden, D. B. op. cit., 321, Fig. 5A; Whimster, J. Archaeology of Surrey (1931), 90 and Pl. 5.

7. We are indebted to Birmingham City Museum for providing us with information about this object.

8. Jacobsthal, P. 'Rhodische Bronzekannen aus Hallstattgräbern', Jahrb. des Deutschen Arch. Inst. 44, 1929, 198-223.

9. Schiek, A. 'Das Hallstattgrab von Vilsingen', in Tubinger Beitrage zur Vor- und Frühgeschichte, Festschrift fur Peter Goessler (1954), 150-167.

10. Kimmig, W. and W. Rest 'Ein Fürstengrab der spaten Hallstattzeit von Kappel am Rhein', Jahrb. des Romisch-Germanischen Zentralmuseums Mainz 1, 1954, 181, Abb. 1,1; 182, No. 10; 207.

11. Déchelette, J. 'Les Récentes Découvertes Préhistoriques en France', Prähistorische Zeitschrift 2, 1910, 209; see also Benoît, F. 'Relations de Marseilles Grecque avec le Monde Occidental', Rivista di Studi Liguri 22, 1956, 8-9 and ibid., 'Recherches sur l'Hellénisation du Midi de la Gaule', Publications des Annales de la Faculté des Lettres Aix-en-Provence (1956) Pl. 2.

12. Benoît, F. 'Recherches', Pl. 2.

13. Frey, O. -H. 'Zu den "rhodischen" Bronzekannen aus Hallstattgräbern', Marburger Wincklemann-Programm 1963, 18-26. He mentions other Italian examples, including one in Paris.

14. Den Boesterd, M. H. P. The Bronze Vessels in the Rijksmuseum G. M. Kam at Nijmegen (1956), 66f., No. 231 with Pl. X, 231-231a.

15. Camporeale, G. I Commerci di Vetulonia in Età Orientalizzante (1969), 108.

16. Garcia y Bellido, A. 'Algunas Novedades Sobre la Arqueologia Punico-Tartessia', Archivo Español de Arqueologia 43, 1970, 31-35; Garrido Roiz, J. P. Excavaciones en la Necropolis de "La Joya", Huelva, Excavaciones Arqueologicas en España 71, 1970, 23-28 with Fig. 12-16.

17. Frey, O. -H., op. cit.

18. See also Dehn, W. and O. -H. Frey 'Die absolute Chronologie der Hallstatt- und Frühlatènezeit Mitteleuropas auf Grund des Südimports', in Atti del VI Congresso Internazionale delle Scienze Preistoriche e Protostoriche - Vol. 1, Relazione generali, (1962), 201.

19. 'Exotic finds in Britain', Antiq. Journ. 15, 1935, 354 with Pl. LIII.

20. Boon, G. C. 'A Greek Vase from the Thames', Journ. Hellenic Studies 74, 1958, 178.

21. Harden, D. B. op. cit., 323 with Fig. 7. Information that it is now lost furnished by Worthing Museum.

22. Higgins, R. A. Catalogue of the Terracottas in the British Museum (1954), 303 and p. 152.

23. Jacobsthal, P. and A. Langsdorff Die Bronzeschnabelkannen (1929).

24. Frey, O. -H. 'Die Zeitstellung des Fürstengrabes von Hatten in Elsass', Germania 35, 1957, 229-49.

25. Frey, O. -H. op. cit. (1957).

26. Szilágyi, J. Gy. 'Zur Frage des Etruskischen Handels nach dem Norden', Acta Antiqua Academiae Scientiarum Hungaricae 1, 1951-52, 422-24.

27. Sharp, S. 'An Account of Roman Remains found at Duston in Northamptonshire', Archaeologia 43, 1871, 118-30.

28. Frey, O. -H. op. cit. (1957).

29. Giessler, R. and Kraft, G. 'Untersuchungen zur frühen und älteren Latènezeit am Oberrhein und in der Schweiz', 32. Bericht Römisch-German. Kommission, 1942-1950, 35, Abb. 7, 10.

30. Brown, W. Ll. The Etruscan Lion (1960), 128-30.

31. Babelon, E. and Blanchet, J. -A. Catalogue des Bronzes Antiques de

la Bibliothèque Nationale (1895), 583, No. 1446

32. Magi, F. *La Raccolta Benedetto Guglielmi nel Museo Gregoriano Etrusco II* (1941), 190, No. 29 with Tav. 58.

33. Schumacher, K. *Grossherzogliche Vereinigte Sammlungen zu Karlsruhe* (1890), 99, No. 534.

34. Helbig, W. in *Annali dell 'Instituto di Corrispondenza Archaeologica* 52, 1880, Tav. U; *Monumenti Antichi* 22, 1913, 558, Fig. 205.

35. Brown, W. Ll. op. cit., 118.

36. Riis, P. J. 'The Bronze Statuette from Uffington, Berkshire', *Journ. Roman Studies* 36, 1946, 43-47 with Pl. VII. It is to be noted that Riis pointed out that the object has a good, even patina of a sort that it would have been unlikely to have acquired had it lain for any length of time in the field where it was found.

37. Dale, W. 'Discovery of a Bronze Bucket... at Weybridge', *Proc. Soc. Antiq. London* 21, 1906-07, 464; *British Museum Guide to Early Iron Age Antiquities* (1925), 91, Fig. 89; Whimster, D. C. *The Archaeology of Surrey* (1931) 90f. with Pl. V; Harden, D. B. op. cit., 319.

38. Stjernquist, B. 'Ett Svenskt Praktfynd med Sydeuropeiske Bronser', in *Proxima Thule* (1962), 72-93; ibid., *Ciste a Cordoni* (1967) II, 30, No. 44 with Pl. XIII, 5 and Pl. XLII, 1.

39. *Inventaria Archaeologica*, Belgium 6.

40. Hencken, H. O'N. *The Archaeology of Cornwall and Scilly* (1932), 178; Fox, A. *South-West England* (1964), 116.

41. Megaw, J. V. S. 'The Vix Burial', *Antiquity* 40, 1966, 43 n.

42. Fox, A. in *Proc. Devon Assoc.*, 1956, 216; Fox, A. op. cit. (1964), 116.

43. *British Museum Guide to Early Iron Age Antiquities* (1925), 92 with Fig. 90.

44. Haverfield, F. 'A Small Bronze Vessel said to have been Found at Bath', *Proc. Soc. Antiq. London* 20, 1903-05, 265-67.

45. Haverfield, F. op. cit.

46. Heron-Allen, E. *Selsey Bill* (1911), 85 and Pl. XVIII.

47. Blegen, C., H. Palmer and R. Young *Corinth XIII, The North East Cemetery* (1964), passim.

48. Robinson, D. M. *Olynthus, Vases found in 1934 and 1938* (1950), 426.

49. Broneer, O. *Corinth IV, Pt. 2, Terracotta Lamps* (1930), 185 and Pl. IV.

50. Harden, D. B., op. cit., 322 with Fig. 6.

51. For the type, see Robinson, D. M. op. cit., 312.

52. Robinson, D. M. op. cit., 255.

53. Howland, R. H. The Athenian Agora IV; Greek Lamps and Their Survivals (1958) 59 and Pl. 37.

54. Broneer, O. op. cit., Pl. 3.

55. Harden, D. B. op. cit., 322 gives the findspot as 'Shotover Hill'. The Ashmolean Museum records only mention 'Shotover Estate'.

56. Howland, R. H. op. cit., 74 (Type 25B) and Pl. 38; Broneer, O. op. cit., Type VII, Pl. 4.

57. Information from Guildhall Museum in litt.

58. Harden, D. B. op. cit., 323.

59. Information in litt. from Warrington Museum.

60. Waddington, Q. op. cit., 386.

61. Haynes, D. E. L. 'An Arrowhead from Cyrene', British Museum Quarterly 24, 1952, 56.

62. Haynes, D. E. L. loc. cit.

63. Snodgrass, A. M. Early Greek Arms and Armour (1964), 147.

64. A very useful list of these imports dating from the late 6th and the whole of the 5th century B. C. is given in Frey, O.-H. 'Importazioni Etrusche della Fine del VI a Tutto il V Sec. nei Territori a Nord delle Alpi', in Mostra dell 'Etruria Padana e della Città di Spina, II, Repertori (1960), 147-52.

65. Jehl, M. and C. Bonnet 'Nouvelles Fouilles et Importantes Trouvailles dans la Forêt du Kastenwald près de Colmar', Cahiers Alsaciens d'Archéologie, d'Art et d'Histoire 1, 1957, 19-28; see also Hatt, J. J. in Gallia 14, 1956, 294-97 and 'Zehn Jahre archäologischer Forschung in Elsass (1946-1956)', Germania 37, 1959, 224-25; Frey, O.-H. Entstehung der Situlenkunst. Die ältere figürlich verzierte Toreutik von Este, Römisch-Germanische Forschungen 31 (1969) 62-63.

66. Dehn, W. and Frey, O.-H. op. cit., 200.

67. Dehn, W. 'Die Bronzeschüssel aus den Hohmichele, Grab VI, und Ihr Verwandtenkreis', Fundberichte aus Schwaben, N. F. 17, 1965, 126-34; ibid. 'Hohmichele Grab 6 - Hradenin Grab 28 - Vace (Watsch) Helmgrab, Ein Nachtrag zu den späthallstättischen Bronzeschüsseln', Fundberichte aus Schwaben, N. F. 19, 1971, 82-88; Frey, O.-H. 'Zu den "rhodischen" Bronzekannen aus Hallstattgräbern', Marburger Winckelmann-Programm 1963, 18-26.

68. Jucker, H. 'Bronzehenkel und Bronzehydria in Pesaro', Studia Oliveriana 13-14, 1965-66, 1-128.

69. Cahn, H. A. 'Le Vase de Bronze de Graechwil et autres Importations Méridionales en Suisse avant les Romains', in Actes du Colloque sur

les Influences Helléniques en Gaule, Publications de l'Université de Dijon, 16 (1958), 21-29.

70. Millotte, J. P. Le Jura et les Plaines de Saone aux Ages des Métaux, Annales Littéraires de l'Université de Besançon 59 (Archéologie 16) (1963), 214.

71. Inventaria Archaeologica, France 1.

72. Joffroy, R. Le Trésor de Vix (Côte-d'Or), Mon. et Mem. Piot 48 (1954).

73. Frey, O.-H. 'Die Zeitstellung des Fürstengrabes von Hatten in Elsass', Germania 35, 1957, 229-49.

74. Jacobsthal, P. 'Bodenfunde griechischer Vasen nördlich der Alpen', Germania 18, 1934, 14-19; Reim, H. 'Zur Henkelplatte eines attischen Kolonettenkraters vom Uetliberg (Zurich)', Germania 46, 1968, 274-85 (distribution map 277, Abb. 1); Schultze-Naumburg, F. 'Eine griechische Scherbe vom Ipf bei Bopfingen/Württemberg', in Marburger Beiträge zur Archäologie der Kelten, Festschrift Dehn, Fundberichte aus Hessen, Beiheft I (1969), 210-12; Kimmig, W. and E. Gersbach 'Die Grabungen auf der Heuneburg 1966-1969', Germania 49, 1971, 24-60; Schweitzer, R. 'Découverte de tessons attiques à figures noires au Britzgyberg près d'Illfurth', Bull. de Musée Hist. Mulhouse 79, 1971, 39-44.

75. Dehn, W. 'Frühe Drehscheibenkeramik nördlich der Alpen', Alt-Thüringen 6, 1962-63, 372-82.

76. Lérat, L. 'L'Amphore de Bronze de Conliège', in Actes du Colloque sur les Influences Helléniques en Gaule, Publications de l'Université de Dijon (1958), 89-98; Millotte, J. P. and M. Vignard. Catalogue des Collections Archéologiques de Lons-le-Saunier, II, Les Antiquités de l'Age du Fer, Annales Littéraires de l'Université de Besançon 48 (Archéologie 13) (1962), 19f. with Pl. 7-10.

77. Kimmig, W. 'Bronzesitulen aus dem Rheinischen Gebirge Hunsrück-Eifel-Westerwald', 43-44. Bericht der Römisch-Germanischen Kommission, 1964, 31-106.

78. Tierney, J. J. 'The Celtic Ethnography of Posidonius', Proc. Royal Irish Academy 60 C, 1960, 247.

79. The most recent list of oenochoai is given in Frey, O.-H. Entstehung der Situlenkunst. Die ältere figürlich verzierte Toreutik von Este, Römisch-Germanische Forschungen 31 (1969), 115-17 with Abb. 49. Others published more recently include those from Tarquinia (Boulomié, B. 'Les Oenochoés à bec en bronze des musées d'Etrurie Centrale et Méridionale', Mélanges d'Archéologie et d'Histoire de l'Ecole Française de Rome 81, 1968, 399f. Information Frey. Unfortunately, this work was not available to us for study in the preparation of this monograph.) and Campli (Teramo) - necropolis of Campovalano (ed. V. Cianfarani, Antiche civiltà d'Abruzzo (1969), No. 90 and 91 with Tav. 39-41. Information Frey) in Italy, two from

Mailhac (Aude) (Taffanel, O. and J. 'Trois Bronzes de Type Etrusque à Mailhac (Aude)', Revue Archéologique de Narbonnaise 3, 1970, 21-31) and another specimen from Eastern France (Harbison, P. 'Une Oenochoe étrusque provenant de l'Est de la France dans une collection privée d'Irlande', Revue Archéologique de l'Est et du Centre Est 23, 1972, 37-43), though see Boulomié, B. 'Les Oenochoés en Bronze du Type Schnabelkanne en France et en Belgique', Gallia 31, 1973, 1-35. There is another from Castaneda in Switzerland (Primas, M. 'Eine Bronzeschnabelkanne des Tessiner Typus aus Castaneda', Jahrb. d. Schweizer. Gesellschaft für Urgeschichte 54, 1968/69, 61-68 and ibid. 'Zwei Etruskische Bronzekannen aus Castaneda', Helvetia Archaeologica 6, 1971, 49-54) and a further example from Worms-Herrnsheim (Schaaff, U. 'Ein keltisches Fürstengrab von Worms-Herrnsheim', Archäologisches Korrespondenzblatt 1, 1971, 107 with Taf. 20). J.-P. Mohen has also informed us of the presence in the Musée des Antiquités Nationales in St. Germain-en-Laye of the handle of an oenochoe found in Du Chatellier's excavations in Saint-Jean-Trolimon (Finistère) (Inv. No. 75.743) and a bronze palmette from Meulan (Yvelines) (Inv. No. 8.509), the latter of which may have formed part of an oenochoe possibly of Etruscan origin (mentioned in Jacobsthal, P. Early Celtic Art (1944) 140).

80. Schaaff, U. 'Versuch einer regionalen Gliederung frühlatènezeitlicher Fürstengräber' in Marburger Beiträge zur Archäologie der Kelten, Festschrift Dehn, Fundberichte aus Hessen, Beiheft I (1969), 187-202. See also Thill, G. 'Frühlatènezeitlicher Fürstengrabhügel bei Altrier', Hémecht 4, 1972, 487-501.

81. Aus'm Weerth, E. Der Grabfund von Wald-Algesheim (1870); Lindenschmidt, L. Alterthümer unserer heidnischen Vorzeit 3, Heft 1, Taf. 1-2; Zahlhaas, G. 'Der Bronzeeimer von Waldalgesheim', Hamburger Beiträge zur Archäologie 1, 2, 1971, 115-29.

82. Freiherr von Tröltsch, E. Fundstatistik der Vorrömischen Metallzeit im Rheingebiete (1884), 60-61.

83. Den Boesterd, M. H. P. The Bronze Vessels in the Rijksmuseum G. M. Kam at Nijmegen (1956), 62-63, Nos. 218-219 with Pl. X, 218. Compare also the unprovenanced handle No. 220 with Pl. X, 220.

84. Den Boesterd, M. H. P. op.cit., Pl. X, 214.

85. Dehn, W. op. cit. in note 67.

86. De Laet, S. J. and W. Glasbergen De Voorgeschiedenis der Lage Landen (1959), 162 with Pl. 37. This was mistakenly given as being a La Tène chariot in Harbison, P. 'The Chariot of Celtic Funerary Tradition', in Marburger Beiträge zur Archäologie der Kelten, Festschrift Dehn, Fundberichte aus Hessen, Beiheft I (1969), 35-36 and 56.

87. Van Doorselaer, A. in Annales 41. Congrès Fédération Archéol. et Hist. Belgique, Malines 1970, 11ff., part. 18; ibid., Kemmel: Attisch aardewerk, Archéologie 1970, 1, p. 21.

88. See note 38.

89. Brøndsted, J. Danmarks Oldtid. III. Jernalderen (1940) 88 and 343; Jacobsthal, P. Early Celtic Art (1944), 139, note 5, and p. 212.

90. Harden, D. B. op. cit., 320.

91. Armand-Calliat, L. 'Un Bassin Mérovingien en Bronze et de Style Copte, trouvé près de Chalons-sur-Saône', Mémoires de la Société des Antiquaires de France, N. S. 4 (Vol. 84), 1969, 65.

92. For map and general discussion, see Harden, D. B. op. cit., 315-19.

93. Kendrick, T. D. and C. F. C. Hawkes Archaeology in England and Wales (1931), 169; Fox, C. Archaeology of the Cambridge Region (1923), 74.

94. Ridgeway, W. and R. A. Smith op. cit., 111.

95. Ridgeway, W. and R. A. Smith loc. cit.

96. Kendrick, T. D. and C. F. C. Hawkes loc. cit.

97. Harden, D. B. op. cit., 316. That Central European fibulae also went southwards over the Alps in the sixth century B.C. has recently been shown by Frey, O. -H. 'Fibeln vom westhallstättischen Typus aus dem Gebiet südlich der Alpen' in Oblatio, Raccolta di Studi di Antichità ed Arte in onore del Prof. Aristide Calderini (1971), 355-86.

98. Clarke, R. R. 'The Iron Age in Norfolk and Suffolk', Archaeol. Journ. 96, 1939, 31.

99. Harden, D. B. op. cit. 316.

100. British Museum Guide to the Early Iron Age Antiquities (1925), Fig. 84. This has a close parallel from Court-St. -Etienne in Belgium, on the same trade route - see Mariën, M. E. Trouvailles du Champ d'Urnes et des Tombelles hallstattiennes de Court-St. -Etienne (1958), 188, n. 5 and 143, n. 8.

101. Hemp, W. F. 'The Clynnog Collar and the Carnguwch Cairn', Arch. Cambrensis 86. part 2, 1931, 354-55.

102. Armstrong, E. C. R. 'A Bronze Bracelet of Hallstatt Type, said to have been found near the town of Antrim', Journ. Royal Soc. Antiq. Ireland 41, 1911, 58-60; ibid. 'The Early Iron Age, or Hallstatt Period in Ireland', Journ. Royal. Soc. Antiq. Ireland 54, 1924, 124-25. Compare also Jope, E. M. 'A Heavy Bronze Ring of Italic Type from Co. Derry', Ulster Journ. of Archaeology 21, 1958, 14-16.

103. Smith, R. A. 'Scarborough and Hallstatt', Antiq. Journ. 14, 1934, 301-02.

104. Coles, J. 'Scottish Late Bronze Age Metalwork: Typology, Distributions and Chronology', Proc. Soc. Antiq. Scotland 93, 1959-60, 16-135 esp. 40ff.

105. Crawford, O. G. S. and R. E. M. Wheeler 'The Llynfawr and other Hoards of the Bronze Age', Archaeologia 71, 1921, 133-40; Fox, C.

and H. A. Hyde 'A Second Cauldron and an Iron Sword from the Llyn Fawr Hoard', <u>Antiq. Journ.</u> 19, 1939, 376-404.

106. Brewster, T. C. <u>The Excavation of Staple Howe, Yorkshire</u> (1963), 115-17. In connection with Hallstatt imports in Britain, reference should also be made to Hawkes, C. F. C. and M. A. Smith 'On Some Buckets and Cauldrons of the Bronze and Early Iron Age', <u>Antiq. Journ.</u> 37, 1957, 131-98, esp. 196-98. See also Hawkes, C. F. C. 'The ABC of the British Iron Age' in Frere (Ed.) <u>Problems of the Iron Age in Southern Britain</u> (n. d. but 1961), 1-16, esp. 9-11. For Scotland, see MacKie, E. W. 'Radiocarbon Dates and the Scottish Iron Age', <u>Antiquity</u> 43, 1969, 15-30, esp. 16 and Piggott, S. 'A Scheme for the Scottish Iron Age' in Rivet (Ed.) <u>The Iron Age in North Britain</u> (1966), 1-17, esp. 6.

107. Sundwall, J. <u>Die Älteren Italischen Fibeln</u> (1943), 239.

108. Sundwall, J. <u>op. cit.</u> 118.

109. Ridgeway, W. and R. A. Smith <u>op. cit.</u> 104. The scarab is regarded as being probably a Roman import in Harris, E. and J. R. <u>The Oriental Cults in Roman Britain,</u> (1965) 91.

110. Boardman, J. <u>The Greeks Overseas</u> (1964), 129.

111. 'Exotic Finds in Britain', <u>Antiq. Journ.</u> 15, 1935, 354 with Pl. LIV.

112. Jacobsthal, P. 'An Iberian Bronze Found at Sligo', <u>Journ. Royal Soc. Antiq. Ireland</u> 68, 1938, 51-54 with Pl. I.

113. Boucher, S. 'Importations étrusques en Gaule à la fin du VIIe siècle avant J. -C.', <u>Gallia</u> 28, 1970, 197, Fig. 7.

114. Dehn, W. ' "Transhumance" in der westlichen Späthallstattkultur ?' <u>Archäologisches Korrespondenzblatt</u> 2, 1972, 125-27.

115. Fischer, F. KEIMHΛIA, Bemerkungen zur kulturgeschichtlichen Interpretation des sogenannten Südimports in der späten Hallstatt - und frühen Latène-Kultur des westlichen Mitteleuropa', <u>Germania</u> 51, 1973, 436-59. See 437, n. 2 for further literature on imports.

116. Piggott, C. M. 'An Iron Age Barrow in the New Forest', <u>Antiq. Journ.</u> 33, 1953, 14-21.

117. See note 4 above.

118. Cunliffe, B. <u>Excavations at Winchester, 1949-60</u> I (1965), 75.

119. Giot, P. R. <u>Brittany</u> (1960), 173.

120. Blanchet, A. 'Recherches sur l'influence commerciale de Massalia en Gaule et dans l'Italie septentrionale', <u>Revue Belge Num.</u> 1913, 318.

121. Cary, M. 'The Greeks and Ancient Trade with the Atlantic', <u>Journ. Hellenic Studies</u> 74, 1924, 178.

122. Birchall, A. 'Aylesford Revisited', <u>British Museum Quarterly</u> 28, 1964, 2; ibid. 'The Aylesford-Swarling Culture, the Problem of the

Belgae Reconsidered', _Proceedings of the Prehistoric Society_ 31, 1965, 241-368, esp. 289.

123. Birchall, A. op. cit., (1965), 289.

124. Werner, J. 'Die Bronzekanne von Kelheim', _Bayerische Vorgeschichtsblätter_ 20, 1954, 43-73.

125. Birchall, A. op. cit., (1965), 289.

126. Smith, R. A. 'On Late Celtic Antiquities discovered at Welwyn, Herts.', _Archaeologia_ 53, 1912, 1-30. See also Stead, I. M. 'A La Tène III Burial at Welwyn Garden City', _Archaeologia_ 101, 1967, 1-62 esp. 44ff.

127. Toynbee, J. M. C. _Art in Britain under the Romans_ (1964), 41.

128. Wheeler, R. E. M. _Rome Beyond the Imperial Frontiers_ (1955, Pelican ed.), 95.

129. Smith, R. A. op. cit. (1912), 16.

130. Wheeler, R. E. M. op. cit., 95.

131. Toynbee, J. M. C. op. cit., 41.

132. Stead, I. M. op. cit. (1967); Hodson, F. R. 'Cultural Grouping within the British Pre-Roman Iron Age', _Proceedings of the Prehistoric Society_ 30, 1964, 99-110, esp. 102.

133. Stead, op. cit., (1967).

www.ingramcontent.com/pod-product-compliance
Lightning Source LLC
Chambersburg PA
CBHW040903240426
43668CB00024B/2454